soul
restoration

The original you is still in there.

melody ross

Melody Ross Media & Soul Road Media, LLC
519 Bird Ave.
Nampa, Idaho 83686
www.melodyrossmedia.com

This workbook is a companion to the teachings of Soul Restoration by Melody Ross. This is a paid course and must be taught by a Soul Road Certified Instructor or online at Soul Road University. The teachings in this workbook are incomplete and must be accompanied by the teachings of your instructor. If you are using this workbook without either a certified instructor or an online membership in Soul Road University to take the course directly from Melody Ross, you are in violation of the terms of this course. You can find a Certified Instructor at SoulRoadMedia.com

Publisher's disclaimer
The information presented in this work is in no way intended as medical advice or as a substitute for medical or professional mental health care. The ideas and information should be used in combination with the guidance and care of your mental health professional if needed. If you are under the care of a mental health professional, you should consult your practitioner before you begin this program. The author and publisher expressly disclaim responsibility for any adverse effects arising from the use or application of information contained in this book.

Printed in the United States of America
First Printing, 2016

Published by Soul Road Media, LLC
www.melodyrossmedia.com

Contents

restore
v.

1. to bring back,
to reinstate

2. to return

3. to repair or renovate
(as in a work of art)
so as to return it to
its original condition

Closing for Restoration

What Does it Mean to *Close* for *Restoration?*

When it is time to restore something valuable, important and irreplacable...there is no detail that is too lavish to take into consideration.

In this case YOU are what is valuable, important and irreplacable. For this restoration...everything has to be moved out of your "Soul House" so that the important work of restoring can be done carefully and thoroughly.

This means, starting now....every voice in your head, every relationship, every opinion, every obligation, every label has to go so that you can hear your own truth.

Everyone has to go but you and your Truthteller

This first step is very important. Even the people you love need to go...this work is just for you, and it is time for you to remember who you are. Once the restoration is done...YOU get to decide who and what is allowed to come close to you or back into your Soul House.

Everyone will be okay. They all have Soul Houses too. You don't have to tell anyone...this is a decision that you make in your mind and heart. It is time for you to rediscover the miracle of you. It is time for you to really know who you are and know of the beautiful life meant for you.

Truth vs. Lies

One of the reasons that many of us spin in circles trying to make our lives work or spend countless resources trying to heal from wounds, yet find ourselves still wounded, is that we are often trying to organize our lives around things that have never been true.

How can we heal from something that was never true to begin with? We can only work with what is real.

We live in a world that does a brilliant job of leading us to believe things that simply aren't true. We are taught that aging is bad, that anger is bad, that sadness is bad....that to feel uncomfortable is bad. Often we believe that if we are any of these things, we ourselves are bad.

We are taught that things should come easily and do come easily if you are using the right lotion or potion or program. Our consumer society urges us to believe that we have some kind of deep void that makes us incomplete, or our relationships incomplete...and that if we would only buy this or try this or do this....and keep buying it and doing it...that we can finally be good enough. We are lied to so that we will never feel good enough, so that we will keep feeling the need to find and buy the next thing that will make us feel good enough.
It is hard to distinguish what is true from what isn't.

So what does the truth feel like? What does it look like? Where do we find it? What does it sound like? Where does it come from? How do we cling to it?

The truth is so much like light, and lies are so much like darkness. Light is something and darkness is nothing. Darkness is literally a lack...a lack of light. It is a void. It is empty. It is nothing. As soon as light is introduced into a dark room...no matter how big the darkness is and no matter how small the light is...as soon as you introduce the light, there is no more darkness. It was never anything to begin with. It just convinced you that it was. So many of us are afraid of the dark, when what we are truly afraid of is the lack of light.

So if light is like truth....then darkness is like lies. To eliminate the lies, we must introduce the truth. The lies cannot survive when the truth shows up.

TRUTH	LIES
Light	Darkness
Authentic	Counterfeit
Real	Fake
Loving	Terrorizing
Growing	Stagnating
Becoming	Reverting
Grace	Condemnation
Clarity	Confusion
Belonging	Rejecting
Progressing	Staying stuck
Equipped	Lacking
Forgiving	Accusing
Calming	Scaring
Accepting	Refusing
Encouraging	Criticizing
Powerful	Powerless
At peace with self	At war with self

Your Soul House

Imagine yourself as a house...with each room in your house holding different parts of yourself. Imagine that when you were born, your soul was put into the beautiful, authentic, resilient, well-built, strong, clean and pure house that is you. This is the real you. You are still in there. The original, incredible you is still in there...though it may feel as though you can not find her.

Things happen in life that make us forget who we are. We are told lies, and we even make up lies to help our lives make sense. We are sometimes used and abused. We make mistakes. Things happen that are out of our control. Our minds begin to believe that those things happen because it is who we are. Our stories sometimes lie to us and people sometimes lie to us. We believe those lies, and our Soul House falls into disrepair.

Often we know that we don't feel right, or that we don't feel like ourselves or that we feel disconnected from ourselves, but we don't know what is wrong or how to fix it. When things have happened that have made us believe lies about ourselves, over time we allow people and situations and habits into our lives that chip away at us. We stop believing that we are valuable enough to protect so we don't learn tools to protect ourselves. Or we have no boundaries and we let everyone in to take our time and our hearts, or to use up and rearrange who we are.

It may feel as though there is no room left for us in our own Soul House, or we may have boarded up our doors and windows to protect ourselves until the light cannot even get in. We may have just shoved all of the things we don't want to remember or think about or face into different rooms of our Soul House and shut and locked those doors. We may just be on autopilot, letting others make our decisions for us, because we have forgotten who we are.

When life goes by for many years this way, we often end up thinking we are broken or destroyed....sometimes we may even believe we are beyond repair.

The lies we believe about who we are and what has happened to us eat away at us...often leaving us feeling like a crack house, believing there is no chance of ever restoring back to who we really are and who we have always been. But we can restore.

If it is the lies that have broken us down and even seemingly destroyed parts of us...it is the truth that will restore us.

We just have to tell ourselves the truth. But first, we have to identify the lies we have believed. We have to be brave enough to do whatever it takes to reach in and rescue the parts of us that are feeling lost.

It is time.
It is time to close for restoration.

If it is the *lies* that have destroyed you... it is the *truth* that will restore you.

Feeling like a "crack house"?

It may seem like a completely overwhelming task to "change" into what we are supposed to be, especially when we feel like such a mess inside.

We don't have to change. We just have to restore. We have to dive in and do a rescue mission, of ourselves. We have to figure out the source of the disrepair and destruction and remove it and then we have to spend some time renovating our soul with what is true.

The truth is, we are never too broken. We are never too used up. We have never made too many mistakes to be able to go back to who we are meant to be and who we have always been. We are meant to be who we were before we started believing lies about ourselves. You are meant for a beautiful life, you always have been.

Your clean, beautiful, original
Soul House

This is who you are.

What if you could strip away everything that is not you, until all that is left is the truth of who you are? You are a soul with a body. You are a soul who is learning, growing and becoming. You are a soul who has lived through countless experiences, each one teaching you something new and adding to the wisdom you have earned throughout your life.

We get to keep all of the lessons we've learned from each of our experiences, and we get to discard all of the lies that we may have told ourselves about those experiences, or that others have told us about our experiences. Once we get rid of the things that are not true...and we invite and embrace the beautiful things about ourselves and life that ARE true...we will restore.

You are good. You always have been. You are true. You are worthy. You are valuable. You are important. Your life matters. You matter.

And just like all of us....some lies have crept in along the way, big and small. Now it's time to dig in and clean out those lies and get back to who you really are. Don't worry...you won't have to do it alone. Everything will change when you shine a light on the darkness. Let's get started....

JOURNALING QUESTIONS

1. Who was I before I started believing
   lies about myself?

2. In what ways do I feel like a crack house?

3. I'm closing for restoration because...

4. I am tired of feeling....

5. I am tired of pretending...

6. I am tired of hiding...

7. I am tired of putting up with...

8. I am tired of thinking about...

9. I want to feel...

10. I want to believe...

11. I want to remember...

12. I want to restore back to...

confidence
strength
happiness
powerful
free
peaceful
energetic
driven
motivated
decisive
authentic
genuine
intuitive
brave
trusting
selfless
loyal
committed
courteous
kind
full of grace
loving
beloved
adventurous
joyful
helpful
safe
secure
feeling
freedom
desire
relationships
belief
faith
clarity
ideas
health
vitality
beauty
unity
connection
fun
belonging
capable
centered
at peace

Your Truthteller

The truth is for all of us. It is not for a certain group of people or a certain kind of person. The truth is the source of all creation, of everything good and true. We are all meant to have a connection to truth. How could we survive without it? We have a constant connection, but often we don't realize this, or we have forgotten it, or lies have made us believe that we are not worthy of it or don't have it anymore.

For your restoration journey, your Truthteller will be your guide. Your Truthteller will be part of your restoration team. As you are restoring, it is so important that you have your Truthteller alongside you, because you will be digging in and looking at so many lies. Lies are loud and convincing, but they are not real. Lies are scary in the dark, but the truth will shine a light on them and they will lose their power. Sometimes we have believed lies for so long that we have a hard time not believing them. It would be too overwhelming to look at our lies without our Truthteller beside us.

Your Truthteller will be holding up a giant light for you, as well as comforting you, telling you the truth and strengthening you during this restoration journey. You get to choose whether to turn the light on or turn it off. Please turn it on.

On the following page are the attributes of your Truthteller.

Identifying *My Truthteller*

- My Truthteller has power & knowledge greater than my own
- My Truthteller loves me without strings attached
- My Truthteller is someone I love and believe
- My Truthteller would never hurt me in any way
- My Truthteller will always lead me to the right places
- My Truthteller helps my heart to feel at peace
- My Truthteller knows my strengths
- My Truthteller knows my weaknesses
- My Truthteller knows my talents
- My Truthteller knows my biggest hurts
- My Truthteller knows what feelings are deepest in my heart
- My Truthteller knows my regrets
- My Truthteller knows my desires
- My Truthteller knows my fears
- My Truthteller knows what I have lived through
- My Truthteller knows what I want most out of life
- My Truthteller knows about my mistakes and loves me regardless
- My Truthteller is willing to tell me when I am astray
- My Truthteller is gentle and kind even when redirecting my course
- My Truthteller lets me make choices but wants me to make the best choices
- My Truthteller will never interfere in my life but is always there to help when asked
- My Truthteller knows what is very best for me
- My Truthteller has infinite wisdom that I don't quite have yet
- My Truthteller wants to help me
- My Truthteller will always tell me the truth

Many people choose God or Jesus Christ as their Truthteller, or a guardian angel or deceased grandparent. You can even choose an animal or bird with the attributes you trust to represent your Truthteller. It is best to not choose someone living in your life...we are all on our own journeys and we make mistakes and fail each other sometimes. Your Truthteller needs to be someone who will never fail you, who will never change, and who is available to you always.

Your *Restoration* Team

You've had it all along...

Your Truthteller

Your 80-year-old self

Your 8-year-old self

Your Truthteller is the most important member of your Restoration Team, but the other members are critically important too. You are not alone on this journey. The raw, unjaded intution of your 8-year-old self is still with you to remind you of who you were before life got so messy. Your 80-year-old self is with you too, to cheer you on and remind you of everything that you have to look forward to and work toward.

As you begin digging through your Soul House to clean out what doesn't belong and to rescue, restore and refurbish what does belong...you will not be alone.

We will first be investigating the source of pain, disrepair and destruction. Your Restoration Team will allow you to pull these things out and explain how it has been for you to live with the lies you have believed. Know that they will be listening carefully and with compassion, and once you have completed that part of this process...they will be ready to tell you the truth, remind you of the truth and help you to believe the truth.

What questions do you have for your Restoration Team?

JOURNALING QUESTIONS

1. What do I wish I could ask my 80-year-old self?

2. What do I wish I could tell my 80-year-old self?

3. What do I wish I could ask my 8-year-old self?

4. What do I wish I could tell my 8-year-old self?

5. What do I wish I could ask my Truthteller?

6. What do I wish I could tell my Truthteller?

7. What do I most need to know to feel at peace?

Your Story

............*in your words*

Imagine at this time that your Restoration Team is sitting beside you, ready to just listen with complete empathy and compassion. The next few exercises will take you through all of the rooms of your Soul House to dig out everything that is there.

It is important for this part of your journey to really honor your story. It is important to listen to yourself explain what it has all been like for you. There are parts of your life that perhaps no one has ever known about. There are parts of your life that you stuffed away deep into your rooms and shut the door, to never be opened again. Your Restoration Team is beside you, carefully listening to your review of your life so far from your perspective.

There are parts of your story that you have never been able to grieve, or celebrate, or explain. There are so many experiences that you have lived through that have never been spoken of. There are so many times that you did not have the chance to tell your side of the story.

Now is the time to carefully pull out all of these experiences, one by one...showing them to your Restoration Team. It is the time for you to talk about the things that hurt, the things that confused you, the things that scared you, the things that disappointed you...the things that changed you. It is time for you to talk about the incredible things that you have accomplished!

You get to feel exactly the way that you feel. This is such an important part of healing and such an important part of your restoration. Let yourself feel it all.

Allow your Restoration Team to hear you out. They will listen with love and compassion to the ways that you have understood and processed the experiences of your life...and then, when you are done...they will tell you the parts that you may have forgotten or that maybe you never knew at all. They will tell you the whole truth.

For now...let's move on to the next exercises. Don't be afraid...you are not alone, and every step of your restoration journey will be so worth it.

What has it been like for you?

Your Timeline

Life changed after that...
I changed after that...
What I thought changed after that...
My dreams changed after that...

birth   10 yrs   20 yrs   30 yrs   40 yrs

Your life has been full of incredible experiences. Some of them are great memories, some of them are hard to think about.

There are so many things that you have lived through, survived, built, endured, conquered, lost, found, created, birthed, grieved. Life is full of all of these kinds of experiences. You made it through.

It is important to look back and see how far we have come. It is important to take some time to really give ourselves credit for the roads we've traveled and also to evaluate where our experiences have left us. It is important to remember that we are still going.

We are going to take a look at our experiences...year by year. Make a mark next to the years that were benchmarks in your growth...whether in good ways or difficult ways. Think especially about the years that changed you, the years that hurt you and the years that seem to haunt you. This is where we will find the information we are seeking. This is a time to just gather facts...we are not digging in to relive these experiences...just to document them.

As you think through the years of your life, meet yourself with compassion, congratulation and support. You have traveled quite a journey. So much of it you did on your own. So much of it no one knows about. So much of it was difficult. There were parts you didn't know that you would be able to make it through, and you did. Tell yourself the truth as you think through these years....that all along, you have been learning, growing and becoming. This is a hero's journey.

This timeline will be a map of where to look for what needs to be removed, what needs to be cared for and what needs to be restored.

What I believe changed after that...
How I felt changed after that...
My possibilities changed after that...
I never spoke of it again after that...

50 yrs   60 yrs   70 yrs   80 yrs   90 yrs   110 yrs

What still hurts?

the three hurts

1. Decisions I have made and I am still living with the consequences.

2. Things that have happened that I did not want to happen, and things that did not happen that I desperately wanted to happen (things that were completely out of my control), but I am still living with the consequences.

3. Decisions other people have made, and I am still living with the consequences.

THE BURN BOOK

*You will need an inexpensive notebook for this exercise...you will be writing down every lie that you have ever believed about yourself and your life that is still hurting.

Using your timeline and thinking through "the three hurts", look back and write down every experience you can think of that led to hurt and then the stories and lies that you may be believing because of those experiences using the following prompts:

I am a beautiful soul who lived through the experience of

_____

and it was devastating, it hurt, it sucked. I hated it.

Some of the lies that I have believed since this experience

are _____.

Burn prompts (lies):

I will never be able to...

I will never have...

I do not deserve...

I did not deserve...

I am...

I am not...

I am meant to...

I will never be able to forgive...

I will never heal from...

Life will always be...

I deserve the suffering of...

I deserve to pay for...

Life will never be...

Cleaning out the *Infection*

Working Through Shame & Blame

Shame and blame keep us stuck where we are...but if we find ourselves feeling shame or blame...we can get to the root of a lot of information that will help us know what our souls most yearn for.

Often we have wounds that we have allowed to get deeper and deeper because we have never dealt with them. When we have unresolved feelings, they don't just go away...they go deeper. Old wounds turn to resentment and bitterness.

We can work through and clean out all of the "infections" of our Soul House. We can get to the root of the infection and then apply truth generously and let our wounds heal.

For this exercise....we are going to hear out our grudges. We are going to let ourselves feel angry. We are going to feel sorry for ourselves. We are going to point our fingers outward and say YOU SHOULD HAVE...!

This is definitely not a good place to stay...but you'll see how letting yourself get to the place your mind goes when it feels weakest and most powerless will help you to take your power back.....and to stop blaming and shaming.

Think through all of the times when you should have been protected, stood up for, taught, warned, rescued, forgiven, communicated with....and let's do this.

Using your timeline and burn book as reference, think about the situations in your life that continue to trigger you and bring you to feelings of anger, jealousy, rage, bitterness, resentment and blame.

And then...FINISH THESE PROMPTS*:

- They should have...........so that........
- They should not have...........so that........
- I wish they would have...........so that........
- They should have protected me from..........so that........
- They should have taught me to...........so that........
- They should have showed up and...........so that........
- They should have helped me...........so that........
- They should have told me..........so that........
- I wish they would have given me...........so that........
- I wish they would have provided me with....so that........
- They should see how hard I've tried to.....so that........
- They should notice that...........so that........
- They should apologize for...........so that........
- They should make restitution to me for.....so that........
- They should admit that...........so that........
- They should tell the truth about...........so that........
- I wish she would have...........so that........
- I wish she would see that...........so that........
- She should have...........so that........
- She should have protected...........so that........
- She should have told me...........so that........
- I wish she would have given me...........so that........
- I wish she would have shown me...........so that........
- I wish she would have invited me to.......so that........
- I wish he would have...........so that........
- I wish he would see that...........so that........
- He should have...........so that........
- He should have protected...........so that........
- He should have told me...........so that........
- I wish he would have given me...........so that........
- I wish he would have shown me...........so that........
- I wish he would have invited me to...........so that........

*Make sure you watch the videos or work with your instructor to see how to finish this exercise...don't stay stuck in these feelings.

(This is a continuation of the previous page...)
Cross out "they should have" and write in...

- I can...

- I will...

- I am capable of...

- I take responsibility for...

- I must...

- Now is the time for me to...

- I have the power to...

- Things will change as I...

- My soul is asking me to...

If your sentences don't make sense....add to the front of

them..."Even though...."

(THIS IS YOUR SOUL'S "TO-DO LIST")

*Sometimes after finishing this exercise, we find that there
are things that we still need to grieve. When something
cannot be changed, sometimes it must be treated as a loss and
we must give ourselves time to grieve the loss of what we we
once loved or what we hoped would happen.

JOURNALING QUESTIONS

1. How has blame and bitterness affected my life?

2. How can I take my power back by taking care of myself?

3. Who and what do I need to let off the hook?

4. How does it feel to take my power back by taking
   responsibility for healing and redeeming my voids?

5. How can I make a commitment to myself to let go of
   bitterness, blame & shame and see these as an opportunity
   to know what my soul is needing?

The *Truth* will restore you

We cannot believe the truth and believe a lie at the same time. They are not the same thing, so we have to choose one or the other. It is hard to just change the direction of our beliefs when it has been a habit for so long to believe something, even if it is not true.

This is why we need help. We need help remembering, we need help knowing. We need help being honest with ourselves. We need help looking into dark places where lies live...so that we can pull the truth out of the lies and let the lies go.

We need help as we lay it all out and look at it, good and bad. Otherwise, we will shove it all back where it was. When we are in the middle of a big restoration project, this is the hardest part...the part where you have to pull out the mess and start sorting. This is the part where we have to remember why we started, and how much it will be worth it. This is the part where we have to remember how far we have already come so that we won't feel tempted to go back to where we were.

And this is the part where our Restoration Team steps in to help. Now that we've pulled out the lies and the bitterness, the shame and the blame...it's time to start shining a light on it and telling it the truth. The truth is what will restore you.

It is time to meet with our Restoration Team and hear what they have to say to us and see what they have to give to us.

Restoration Team Meditation

RESTORATION MEDITATION

*Before you begin the meditation, pull out your journal and write down the following questions so that as soon as the meditation is over, you can write down everything you remember from it.

1. What did my 8-year-old self have to say to me?

2. What did she bring me?

3. What did she remind me about?

4. What did my 80-year-old self have to say to me?

5. What did she bring me?

6. What did she remind me about?

7. What did my Truthteller have to say to me?

8. What did my Truthteller bring me?

9. What did my Truthteller remind me about?

10. What do I want to remember forever about meeting with my Restoration Team?

11. How can I keep my Restoration Team with me?

Notes From Your
Restoration Team

Now that you've pulled out the lies that have been wreaking havoc in your Soul House...it's time to take a look at each one and stand up to it...then ask yourself and your Restoration Team what the truth is about each of those lies.

This is where we start to shine a bright light on what is not true. This is where we remove and eliminate what does not belong by replacing it with what does belong. This is where we decide to remember what is true and not true. This is where we begin to restore.

We will be making "Truth Cards" by searching from the truths on the following pages and asking our Truthteller, our 80-year-old self and our 8-year-old self what is true about us. Then, we will cut out those truths and assemble them into individual, personal notes to us called Truth Cards.

As you read through these messages, imagine the members of your team speaking them to you...look them right in the eye and really listen. Read through your Burn Book and identify the lies that you most need to remove from your life, and focus on the truth that shines a light on those lies.

Look back at pages 8-9 to remember what the truth feels like and what lies feel like. Let yourself feel the truth and invite it into your Soul House. Refuse to allow the lies to have power over you anymore.

Let your Restoration Team speak to you with compassion and support, even tenderness. The truth might feel unfamiliar, you may be in the habit of hearing lies. Embrace the truth..once you know the truth, you are no longer powerless. The truth has always been true...and it it has always been meant for you.

Dear Surviving Soul,
You will be able to trust again.
You will be happy again.
Let the door close all the way.
You can start over
right now.

Dear Worthy Soul,
Open your eyes to the help that
shows up for you just in time.
If you have turned away from faith,
turn back again and ask for help.
Let others help.
Let others love you.
Accept their kindness.
It will heal you
and it will heal them.

Dear Hurting Soul,
No more worrying.
Be at peace.
Let your mind rest.
Live as if
you are absolutely beloved
.....Because you are.

Dear Exhausted Soul,
Let them choose. They have to learn
the lessons, too.
Everyone is on their own journey,
learning the truth for themselves.
Let it be.

Benevolent Soul,
time for you to let go of what
been holding you back. It is time.
You really can do this.
You were born for greatness.

Dear Warrior Soul,
You have done the best
you
could do.
Give yourself grace.
You don't have to hustle for
your spot in the world.
You already belong.

Sometimes you forget how much you already know. Please remember.

Sometimes you forget how much you have already accomplished. Please remember.

Tell yourself the truth about everything. It will set you free.

Think of yourself the way you want your loved ones to think of themselves.

Everything circles back around; this will too.

You will know joy again.

You will know happiness again.

Focus on the true things.

Please make time for rest.

Please make time for play.

It is going to be worth it.

You have been through so much. Please give yourself some credit.

You have endured so much. It is okay to be tired.

This has been a hard road, and you made it.

What others have done to you does not define you.

What other people think of you does not define you.

Hard times always pass.

You are not powerless. You can choose.

You have power in this situation. Please use it, dear soul.

You can take your power back.

Your mistakes have taught you valuable things.

You have earned so much wisdom. It is time to use it.

Please don't settle for things that feel wrong.

You don't have to be afraid of being alone.

There is nothing wrong with being alone for a while.

You are infinitely valuable.

You are loved more than you can imagine. You always have been.

Be who YOU are, not anyone else.

You have so much more bravery than you think you do.

You are so much more than you have believed you are.

You are perfectly imperfect, just as you are.

Do not give any more energy to the things you want to be free from.

You are enough today...you don't have to prove anything to anyone.

The good things happening are meant to be, for you.

Please don't compare your life to others, you are incomparable.

Those tough experiences made you stronger...it is time to start using that strength.

You will heal...you are healing right now.

You get to start over today.

Enjoy the things around you; life is meant to be enjoyed.

Look around and be grateful; there is so much to be thankful for.

It is time to stop settling for less.

Be brave enough for honesty.

It's okay to show up exactly as you are, even if you wish you were better.

You are still learning...you will always be learning.

Pain is often a gift...look for the message the pain is bringing.

Anger is a messenger; ask it what it wants you to know.

Protect what needs to be protected.

Fight for what is precious.

Let go what needs to be let go.

It's ok to want things that don't make sense to others.

What if your purpose was to live a joyful life?

Your purpose is to live a joyful life.

Be brave enough to make things right.

Choose the path that is most noble.

Don't you dare give up.

Keep at it...please don't quit.

You can begin again. As many times as it takes.

It is time to move past the past.

The years ahead will be the best ones yet.

Everyone has life seasons; expect it! Good times, hard times, confusing times...nothing stays the same. Be patient and try to learn as much as you can from each one. The seasons will change again when it is time.

Everyone who truly knows you believes in you.

You will fly again...you will soar!

Don't miss out on all of those blessings waiting for you.

Listen to those beautiful messages that have been coming through loud and clear; they really are meant for you.

Nothing matters more than this day, and the choices you make this day.

Miracles will happen for you today.

There are always miracles available to you. Just ask.

Be open to miracles happening in ways that you did not expect.

Grief is real. It lasts as long as it lasts. Then it passes...you will be at peace again. You will get through this.

Your slate is clean.

Put more time into what matters most to you, and less time into what is necessary but drains your energy.

You have what you need to change the parts of your life that are not working...it is time.

You don't have to settle for things that make you feel small and powerless...you always have a choice.

You will never regret standing up for what you believe in...no matter how hard it seems at the time.

Strength comes from resistance. Hard times are a time of growth and strength building.

You can start over right now.

Every minute is a brand new chance to choose another way.

Be kind to your dreams and they will be kind to you.

Give yourself some grace. You are a work in progress.

You are not too damaged to become whole again. You will be whole again.

You will be able to trust again.

You will be happy again.

You will feel strong and brave again.

You can trust. It is going to be okay.

Be patient with yourself. You are learning.

You have done the best you could do. Give yourself grace.

When you know better...you do better. You are learning.

A good life consists of good choices, one after another.

You have the power to choose a happy life.

Some things can not be changed, but you always have the power to choose the way you react to those things.

When there is a prompting or a deep desire in your heart...it's a message from your soul to take action. Please take action, dear soul.

Soul work is hard work, friend. Stick with it. It showed up in your life for a reason, it is time.

You do not travel alone...you have help all around you that you just cannot see.

You will get through this time... you really will.

Let yourself enjoy the good things that happen to you.

It may be going slower than you had planned, or than you wish it would...but it is happening!

You can forgive the atrocities done to you, it will set you free.

You can forgive the abandonment. It will set you free.

You can forgive the betrayal. It will set you free.

You can forgive the abuse. It will set you free.

You can forgive the things withheld from you. It will set you free.

You can forgive yourself. It will set you free.

It was never okay for you to be hurt or abused. It was never okay.

It may feel uncomfortable, it may be difficult...but this is exactly where you need to be for where you want to go.

Make sure they know how much you love them.

If you really want to improve that relationship that means so much to you...put that person's needs and wants ahead of your own. Just try it, friend. It works miracles.

Make sure they know that you are doing this for them, and for you.

It is time to forgive yourself... wholly and completely.

You already know what the answer is. Trust it. It is right.

It is time for you to let go of what has been holding you back. It is time.

No more worrying. Be at peace. Let your mind rest.

Do everything you can to make it right. Then let it go.

Set yourself free. Welcome yourself home. It is time to be uncaged.

You are loved and accepted exactly as you are.

You are wonderful exactly as you are.

You make things better. You make life better.

No one can do it for you. You are worth the sacrifice it is going to take.

If you are still wondering if that miracle that happened in your life was real...it was, and it was meant just for you.

Your life is unfolding for you in perfect ways that you cannot see.

Your wings are unfolding...do you feel it?

It's time to start believing in that secret dream of yours. It is time to start working toward it.

You don't have to hustle for worthiness. You are already worthy.

You don't have to hustle for your spot in the world. You already belong.

Have the patience needed to take the time to make the right decision for yourself.

What's done is done...it is time to move forward.

Let others help. Let others love you. Accept their kindness. It will heal you and it will heal them.

You've got to ask for what you want...but first you've got to know what you want. Be brave enough to take the time to really figure out what you want, and then ask for it.

This is all up to you, dear soul. No one gets to decide for you.

Your painful experiences will help you to understand the pain of others...you will be a miracle to someone else just by telling your story.

Time will heal it....time, love and faith.

Go ahead and dream the dreams that seem impossible...it is the way that you will get to where your heart wants to go.

Someone needs to hear your song. It is time to sing that song that your soul wants to sing. Please don't let it go unsung.

Everything about you is unique and miraculous. It is impossible to compare yourself with others.

Let others be who they are.

Don't let your happiness or peace be dependent on others.

You have come so far...and you will go so much further too.

Someone needs that story in your soul that is aching to be told. Please don't let it die with you.

Everything about you is unique and miraculous. It is impossible to compare yourself with others.

You don't have to take on the whole thing today. All you have to do today is take the first step.

Let others be who they are.

Don't let your happiness or peace be dependent on others.

You have come so far...and you will go so much further too.

You are enough today, right now.

Listen to that voice inside of you that is telling you that it's time to simplify...it is telling you the truth.

It is time to get rid of the poison parts of your life. It is time, you are ready.

You make the world a better place. You really do. Your life makes a difference.

Everything is always on its way to becoming what it is supposed to be next...everything...don't fight it.

Patience is what is required right now...it will be hard, but you can do it. Please don't give up.

You have done a lot of very difficult things in your life, and you can do this too.

You are strong enough, and you are getting stronger every day.

You have made a tremendous difference.

Today is day one. That means no matter what happened yesterday or the day before that, you can start again today being the woman you want to be.

You were born for greatness.

You were born to contribute things that only you can contribute.

You were never meant to fit in... you were meant to shine as a light in the darkness.

You will feel whole again.

You have the courage needed to do this. Dig deep. It is all there.

You have a profound effect on others, just by being who you are.

It is okay to cry, it is okay to hurt, it is okay to be human.

It is ok to feel weak. You will be strong again.

Your life has been blessed. You have been blessed. Accept those blessings as the gifts they were intended to be, meant for you, with the love that was attached to them.

No one will completely understand your pain. You will be able to help others by having and understanding some of their pain...and it will help you to heal too. This is a miracle.

You are getting there...keep going.

Your fire never goes all the way out. You are still in there. Your fire is still in there. Throw a stick on it...blow on it...you will be on fire again before you know it.

Be still. Listen. Be patient. Ask specifically. The answers will come.

Live as if you are absolutely beloved ....because you are.

You are deeply loved exactly as you are...you do not have to earn it.

You have always been loved. It has been with you along.

You have not been forsaken. You do not walk alone.

The world will tell you that happiness comes from more, bigger, better, newer. Find out for yourself if this is true...when you find the truth, you will be brave enough to live that truth.

There are wonderful, kind, supportive, selfless people in the world...lots of them...THESE are the people you deserve to spend your time with. Don't settle for anything less.

It is not too late to change your life...it is never too late. Don't ever let anyone tell you that it is.

You soul doesn't have to change...you just have to restore back to who you have always been.

Don't let those words go unspoken any longer...that apology, that "I love you"...it is time to speak them.

Sometimes the pain will seem more than you can bear. This does not mean that you are weak. This is the time to turn your pain over to your Truthteller.

If they don't know your soul, their opinions of you don't matter.

Betrayals sting....but bitterness and anger will kill you, friend. Time to let it go.

Start the path toward forgiveness, for yourself and your own peace of mind. It will not be easy, but it will be worth it. You do not have to do it alone.

What others do to you has nothing to do with you. Let others own their actions and choose positive responses for your own life. It is difficult, but it is the way to peace.

Life will be beautiful again. Life will be more beautiful than ever.

Your future starts right now. Pack light and leave everything unnecessary behind.

You do not need anything else to move forward. You have the help you need and you have everything else inside of you.

Get back up, dust yourself off and take another step...and then another.

Believe the truth about yourself ...that there is nothing you could ever do or that anyone else could ever do to change how infinitely valuable you are.

You are not replaceable. There is only one you.

Do not let others decide for you. This is your life.

You made it through yesterday, you are making it through today, and you will make it through tomorrow.

Protect your sacred relationships. It is important. It is worth it.

Put your efforts and energy toward things that you want more of...not things you don't even want.

Let the door close all the way.

There is so much ahead for you.

Your future starts right now. Pack light and leave everything unnecessary behind.

You do not need anything else to move forward. You have the help you need and you have everything else inside of you.

Get back up, dust yourself off and take another step...and then another.

Believe the truth about yourself ...that there is nothing you could ever do or that anyone else could ever do to change how infinitely valuable you are.

You are not replaceable. There is only one you.

Do not let others decide for you. This is your life.

You made it through yesterday, you are making it through today, and you will make it through tomorrow. You will.

Protect your sacred relationships. It is important. It is worth it.

Put your efforts and energy toward things that you want more of...not things you don't even want.

Let the door close all the way.

There is so much ahead for you.

Open the good doors that are waiting and meant for you.

Decide to be alive every day.

You are enough. The work you do is enough. The sacrifices you make are enough.

Life really will make sense again.

For every terrible, scary, awful thing happening in the world, there are 100 examples of people being good to each other. We don't hear about them as often, but they're happening all around us.

Forgiving someone has nothing to do with that person, or whether they "deserve" it... it's a gift to yourself, to stop carrying heavy and painful and exhausting stuff around all the time. Forgive, and be free.

Look for what is right in your life rather than what is wrong.

Taking risks is scary... but no matter what happens as a result, you'll be okay--and the greatest treasures in our lives are usually found by stepping just outside our comfort zones.

Remember how good it feels to be home and protect it fiercely.

Be patient with your questions, sometimes it is not time yet for you to know the answers.

Do not lose hope in true love. It is what is meant for you.

You are so loved, dear one. Trust this truth forever.

Someday soon, you will count more good and happy days than sad and difficult ones.

It is so important for you to forgive yourself.

It is time for you to start setting boundaries. No more settling.

There is great strength in admitting your vulnerabilities. Let others love you and help you where you are vulnerable.

You deserve a good life.

You can use your lessons to teach others.

You are powerful.

You are strong.

You really are brave.

You are never, ever alone.

You are heard, you are understood.

Your mistakes are not who you are. Let them go. Forget the mistakes and keep the lessons.

You will be able to trust again.

You do not need the approval or validation of others to live your truth.

Someday you will be thankful for just about every experience you have ever had. Each one has shaped you into the remarkable being that you are.

Your heart is good. You are good.

Walk in your truth, not in the darkness.

It is time to hold your head up high. You made it through.

Things will be peaceful again.

Your tears will not be wasted. Beautiful things will come of them.

When you fall down, you can get back up. You get stronger every time.

You are learning so much. You are becoming so wise.

You have already learned so much.

It might take a few tries. It is okay. Just don't quit, friend.

Every day you are getting stronger, braver, more certain.

It is an act of respect and dignity toward yourself to make and keep boundaries with others.

They need you. You are needed. It is okay to be needed.

It is going to be okay.

Starting over is hard...and you are strong enough to do it.

Be patient, things are being orchestrated on your behalf that you cannot see.

It is okay if some people are in your life for just a little while.

Let them choose. They have to learn the lessons too.

Make your choices count...they are yours and yours alone.

You can be proud of making it to now.

Let those heavy things go.

You may have been lied to...and you may have believed it. You don't have to believe it anymore. Tell yourself the truth. Believe the truth.

You are right where you belong. It is no accident that you are where you are, doing what you are doing, with those you are doing it with. This is a part of your story.

It is time to challenge the lies.

Your story is rich and beautiful... the rough parts are so important.

It is so important that you begin to take care of yourself...body and soul. No one else can do it for you, and it must be done.

Your best is not the same best as anyone else's best....please don't compare...you are incomparable.

It is okay to step back and watch and wait for a little while. It is okay.

Please just trust this time in your life. It is going somewhere.

It is worth every sacrifice to walk in your truth.

Do your best, then let it go.

This day is temporary...new days are ahead.

This part might hurt a little...but it is absolutely necessary. Be brave.

Forgive everyone...yes, everyone.

It keeps showing up for a reason.

Pain has valuable, beautiful lessons...listen closely.

Be kind to your soul.

Be willing to sacrifice...it is worth it, and sometimes it is the only way.

Please stop being a bully to yourself. Be kind to you.

Choose what is best, not just what is good.

Make your Truthteller your companion each day. Walk together. You don't ever have to go through your life alone.

Just start.

The truth will heal this.
The whole truth.

It is okay to go a different way than the way of those around you... as long as it is the way of truth.

It is okay if others do not understand.

Please do not let the destructive words and actions of others into your life.

Being thankful is one of the most important parts of life.

It wasn't your fault. You did not deserve to be treated that way.
No one does.

Do not ever let anything trap you. If you feel trapped...fly free.

What's done is done. It is time to heal.

There are good people all around...there really are.

Look for the good people doing the good things...that is where you belong.

You are made of goodness.

Protect your dreams...keep them sacred until they are strong enough to be in the world.

Someday it won't hurt so much.

A beautiful life is waiting for you to take hold. Believe it.
It will happen as soon as it is time.

It is okay to admit that you were wrong. Everyone is wrong sometimes.

The truth is the truth is the truth.

You get to change your mind.

You have not run out of chances. Life is a journey with a new chance every single day.

You are worthy of love. You are worthy of happiness. You are worthy of all good things.

You have been watched over all along.

They are rooting for you. They believe in you. They are on your side.

Please ask for help.

There is no quota on miracles. You can ask for a miracle today and always.

The debt has been paid.

So much good is waiting for you... no strings attached.

You do not have to pay for every good thing that happens to you.

Please stop punishing yourself.

Please stop letting others punish you and make you suffer.

You know. Trust yourself.

Give yourself some grace.
Give everyone some grace.

Faith ebbs and flows for everyone. Be patient with it. Hold on to it even if it is small.

Your body is not who you are. Bodies age and deteriorate over time. You are a soul. Souls grow and progress and get better and better.
You are a soul.

When bad things happen, don't choose to do things in the moment that numb you but make everything worse. Choose to do things that make your life better.

Always think about how you want to feel at the end of the day....and make decisions that get you there.

Dear Brave Soul,

Dear Beautiful Soul,

Dear Courageous Soul,

Dear Beloved Soul,

Dear Good Soul,

Dear Learning Soul,

Dear Surviving Soul,

Dear Tired Soul,

Dear Grieving Soul,

Dear Fighting Soul,

Dear Warrior Soul,

Dear Gentle Soul,

Dear Strong Soul,

Dear Noble Soul,

Dear Benevolent Soul,

Dear Loving Soul,

Dear Hurting Soul,

Dear Confused Soul,

Dear Feeling Lost Soul,

Dear Happy Soul,

Dear Authentic Soul,

Dear Pure Hearted Soul,

Dear Sorrowful Soul,

Dear Thankful Soul,

Dear Fun Loving Soul,

Dear Thoughtful Soul,

Dear Wondering Soul,

Dear Contemplating Soul,

Dear Hard Working Soul,

Dear Kind Soul,

Dear Daring Soul,

Dear Adventurous Soul,

Dear Heroic Soul,

Dear Fun Loving Soul,

Dear Gutsy Soul,

Dear Brilliant Soul,

Dear Genius Soul,

Dear Honest Soul,

Dear Creative Soul,

Dear Analytical Soul,

Dear Worrying Soul,

Dear Devastated Soul,

Dear Exhausted Soul,

Dear Weary Soul,

Dear Lion Hearted Soul,

Dear Shy Soul,

Dear Afraid Soul,

Dear Bold Soul,

Dear Exceptional Soul,

Dear Worthy Soul,

Dear Honorable Soul,

Dear Dauntless Soul,

Dear Persevering Soul,

Dear Steadfast Soul,

Dear Wobbling Soul,

Dear Wavering Soul,

Dear Enduring Soul,

Dear Tough Soul,

Dear Broken Soul,

Dear Bruised Soul,

Dear Brave Soul,

Dear Beautiful Soul,

Dear Courageous Soul,

Dear Beloved Soul,

Dear Good Soul,

Dear Learning Soul,

Dear Surviving Soul,

Dear Tired Soul,

Dear Grieving Soul,

Dear Fighting Soul,

Dear Warrior Soul,

Dear Gentle Soul,

Dear Strong Soul,

Dear Noble Soul,

Dear Benevolent Soul,

Dear Loving Soul,

Dear Hurting Soul,

Dear Confused Soul,

Dear Feeling Lost Soul,

Dear Happy Soul,

Dear Authentic Soul,

Dear Pure Hearted Soul,

Dear Sorrowful Soul,

Dear Thankful Soul,

Dear Fun Loving Soul,

Dear Thoughtful Soul,

Dear Wondering Soul,

Dear Contemplating Soul,

Dear Hard Working Soul,

Dear Kind Soul,

Restoring
Your Power

No more excuses...

Where do I feel *Powerless?*

Even after we know the truth and call out the lies, often we still have old habits, difficult circumstances and relationships that may make us feel like we can't have the life we want to live. Even when we have eliminated the lies, we still have things in our lives that are true facts that we have to overcome. All of us have hard parts in our lives. We may have people in our lives who are hard to deal with. We may have physical weaknesses to overcome. We may have financial problems to overcome. All of us have a lot of reasons that make it difficult to move forward.

After doing the work of healing, often we still keep behaving as if we are not healed... simply because we don't know how to behave yet. It is hard to deal with the reactions of others as we are trying to change the way we live our life, and it is just flat out hard to change old habits.

There are a lot of things in life that we have no control over...that we cannot change, but there are also a lot of things that we can. Making changes is hard work, but if we want to live the life that we are meant to live...that our souls are meant to live...we are going to have to do some difficult things. Not very many worthwhile things in life come easily; that is why those things mean so much to us. It is worth the work it takes to be true to our souls and live the lives that we are meant to live.

Where do you find yourself thinking "I know the truth about myself but...." or "I get what you are trying to say here, but what you don't know about my life is that..."

What places in your life feel like a big stop sign, or a dam or a huge mountain to climb? Where do you feel powerless?

Let's spend some time thinking about those things.

JOURNALING QUESTIONS

1. What situations do I have in my life that make me feel like I don't have choices?

2. What relationships do I have in my life that make me feel like I don't have choices?

3. What in my life makes me feel trapped?

4. What circumstances do I have in my life that feel like constant hurdles to overcome?

5. What do I wish I did not have to deal with every day?

6. Who do I wish I did not have to deal with every day?

7. What do I wish I had to make my life easier?

8. What are some habits that I wish I could overcome?

9. Where in my life do I feel a heavy weight that keeps me down and makes me feel like I can't move forward?

10. What am I procrastinating because I know how hard it will be?

MY STORY

You might wonder why I teach about restoring of souls so passionately. One of the great gifts of my life is the special knowledge I have about restoring. The thing is, you cannot restore something if it has not been changed or damaged from its original condition, so gaining this knowledge came from a lot of loss and damage and disrepair. I call it a gift because this understanding of what it takes to rise up after you have been knocked down has been the seed of the greatest miracles of my life. I am thankful to know so much about restoring.

I have always been one who dreamed big dreams and I've always been willing to take risks, from the time I was very small. My life was met with the ordinary challenges of every human being...trying to fit in, find my way, realizing maybe I don't want to fit in....bouncing back and forth between wanting to be different and wanting to belong. It is hard to be a human being. I think we forget that sometimes. Along with the ordinary challenges, I have had the opportunity to learn from other intense and painful losses. Loss of myself, loss of what I worked hard to build, loss of relationships, loss of faith, loss of health, loss of love, loss of confidence, loss of hope.

Some things happened in my childhood that made me believe that I was not as valuable as other human beings. I began early on to construct my life around that lie. I literally thought that if you looked deep inside of me, you would find something very bad...so I began to work very hard to make up for that so that I could still have big dreams and still have a good life. I created a system in my mind where I would do extra work, pay extra amounts, be extra good so that I could earn a place in the world with the rest of the people who are not bad like me.

Starting out life as a young person believing a lie requires a lot of unwinding once you learn the truth. My restoring had to go all the way back to that first lie...and I had to unwind every decision I had ever made based on that lie and every story I had ever told myself that validated that lie.

I got married when I was 18. I met someone who saw me as 100% good. He was the best thing that ever happened to me. We immediately started building a family and building our dreams. He bought me paints and paint brushes and listened to my ideas. He believed in me. He even became my Truthteller. He worked hard every day so I could stay home and raise our children and paint and write. He loved to do fun things; he especially loved water sports. So as he would buy me more art supplies whenever he got the chance....my secret dream was to be able to paint enough and write enough so that I could buy him a boat someday.

We started out in a tiny little house; we remodeled it and sold it and bought a little bit bigger tiny house...we remodeled and sold it. We built our first little brand new house. By then, we had 3 children. We were so in love and we worked so hard every day to build our life. I worked hard to be good and pretty and excellent in all things so that I could deserve all of this goodness.

Seven years after we were married, when I was only 25 and he was 28....we started our first business selling books that I wrote. I secretly wrote the books so that I could buy him a boat. It was a big risk and we put everything into it. Within a few years, we were millionaires. We bought a used boat.

Life became sort of a fairy tale for a while after that. I had 2 more babies and we moved to a 100 year old farm. We spent almost a year restoring the house and growing the biggest, greenest lawn you have ever seen. We kept our business on the farm so we could be with our children.

Seven years after we started our business, I had finally saved up enough money to buy my husband his dream boat. Just a few weeks after its maiden voyage, he took our children and a few of our friends to the lake and had a terrible accident. He sustained a traumatic brain injury.

Over the next few years, I became solely responsible for our life. Over the course of those years, we lost our business, our home and pretty much everything we had worked so hard to build together. We lost friends, we lost our identity, we lost each other for a while. We lost it all because life is hard; we lost it all because I made bad decisions, we lost it all because other people made bad decisions; we lost it all because bad things happened that were out of our control.

I was convinced that we lost everything because I was bad.

To move forward, I had to confront the lies. When I lost my husband for all of those years, I lost my Truthteller. I had to learn that my Truthteller is not my husband. I had to learn that I am not bad and that I have never been bad. I had to learn that life is full of difficult challenges and that they are not punishments, but the way to wisdom and truth. I had to learn how powerful our minds are in making up stories to make things make sense. I had to learn to clean out the infection. I had to learn to trust and cling to my actual Truthteller, and that the truth and everything good and true is meant for me, too. I had to learn to clean out the infection. I had to learn to trust myself, trust life and trust the truth. I had to learn to restore.

It took about 7 years for my husband to completely recover. 7 years after his accident, our bankruptcy was final. The date stamped on our bankruptcy closing papers was our 21st wedding anniversary.

A year later I started getting hives all over my body...and it lasted for almost 3 years as my body shut down in adrenal fatigue. I gained almost 50 pounds and lost my vitality and youthful beauty. It was another devastating loss. It was the first time in my life that I didn't believe I was being punished for being bad, but that I just needed to listen to what my body needs from me. I am still on the long journey of restoring my health and my body.

You see, I've had the great gift of having to learn to restore. Just about everything that I valued so much has been taken from me, and when it was possible, I learned to restore it with the help of my restoration team.

I am passionate about teaching restoration because I can not stand to see the pain in my fellow human beings of believing lies about themselves. I know now that NONE of us are unworthy of a good and beautiful life; not me...not you. We are all meant for truth, beauty, love and peace.

Once we know who we are, we begin to behave as if we are beloved, valuable and important. Then we know it is the same for everyone, and we treat others as if they are beloved, valuable and important. It changes everything. It changes the world.

I beg you to take on the edeavor of the work it takes to restore yourself back to who you have always been...to restore your thoughts and your actions and your words to be in alignment with how incredibly valuable you are in this world. It is worth it.

I know it's hard. But you've got to do it anyway. Every hero and heroine throughout history had to do the same. Look your trials in the eye and get up and do it anyway.

All my best to you,
melody ross

She Did It Anyway

This is where you write your story. This is the story of a heroine. A heroine who could not be a heroine without something very difficult to overcome, conquer or rescue.

Think of every person you have ever admired...and what it was about them that you admired. Think of real life heroines and heroes. Think of the every day people who do the right thing, the best thing, the noble thing...in spite of so many difficulties.

This is who YOU are. You are one who can do difficult things. You are one who has already done so many difficult things. You are one who has made hard choices and big sacrifices. You are one who has made mistakes and maybe even messed things up a time or two. You are one who has kept going, or you would not be here today. You are a heroine already.

It would be wonderful if there were an easy way to get to all of the places that we want to go. But if you look back through all of history....this is the way that women and men have gotten where they needed to go, where girls and boys have made it through what they needed to make it through......they looked at their fears, they looked at their hurdles...and they did it anyway.

Let's write your story. The story of a woman who did it anyway.

They didn't support her decisions They told her she was being selfish
They threw fits about it   She felt defeated   She sometimes felt unloved
It seemed that everything she worked for somehow crumbled overnight
She sometimes believed the lies herself She felt alone
She was really mad at herself for a while They were not very kind to her
They did not seem to understand her They did not know what to think of her
They looked at her like she was crazy They yelled at her
They said she could never get past her past They ignored her
They said she would never be able to change He broke her heart
He betrayed her He left her for someone else He belittled her He hurt her
He made her life miserable He tried to keep her from moving forward
He turned people against her There were people with more money
There were people with more experience There were real obstacles
There were imagined obstacles There were people with better connections
There was competition There was no way of knowing if it would work out or not
There seemed to be forces working against her She was furious
She didn't know all of the answers She didn't have everything she needed
She was getting older She didn't have the energy she used to have
She had tried so many times before She was confused She felt blah
She didn't know where the resources would come from
She knew it would be a very long journey She wondered if it really mattered
She knew she might have to do it alone She knew it would take a lot of hard work
They listed all of her past mistakes They would not even listen
They told her that she should just give up   They made fun of her
They made fun of her ideas They laughed at her They did not include her
She didn't know if she could trust them   She had been down this road before
She didn't know how things would turn out She was not always her best
She felt like she may have run out of chances She cried a lot
She screamed She yelled She sometimes lost control completely They accused her
They tried to get her to stop what she was doing She had quit before
She had started before She had already done this a few times before
It gave her a headache sometimes It made her tired sometimes
It was so difficult sometimes It was all very confusing at times
It made her heart hurt sometimes It was so difficult sometimes
It was all very confusing at times It was not easy to keep going
She didn't always want to get up in the morning She sometimes complained
She did not always greet the day with cheerfulness
She did not always have a fabulous attitude about it She cried about it
She had tears in her eyes She did it through bouts of sobbing
She sometimes was not very much fun She had never done it before
She didn't know what she was doing She had started, then quit... repeat
They did everything they could to stop her She did not always want to get back up
She was afraid to let them see who she was capable of becoming
She was afraid of what might happen   She was afraid of being alone
She was afraid of how her life might change She was afraid of them
She was afraid that she could not move past it
She wondered if her ideas were good enough She wondered if she was smart enough
She was afraid that she could never really change
She wondered what she had gotten herself into She stomped her feet
She wondered if she would be able to keep going She knew it would be hard
She wondered if she really had what it would take
She wondered if she really did make a difference in the world
She wondered if she was strong enough She knew she was taking a big risk
She knew she would have to sacrifice She knew heartache

They told her she could never do it They told her it was a ridiculous idea
She was scared They said she was underqualified They said she was too old
She felt underqualified They made it very hard for her She was very tired
The cards seemed stacked against her She threw fits sometimes
She sometimes felt like her best years were over She was devastated
They tried to stop her They told her she was wasting her time
They told her to be normal She felt lonely She felt like an outsider sometimes
She made mistakes She made more mistakes Some people she loved betrayed her
She made some wrong turns Her heart was broken They said it was her fault
They didn't love her back She didn't know all of the answers
She was afraid of getting hurt She was afraid she would fail
They told her she would fail They told her she was too young
She thought others could probably do it better than she could
She had tried it before and not quite made it She was absolutely terrified
They said "who do you think you are, anyway?" She felt angry
She felt like she was pretending to know what she was doing
Everything kept going wrong It was taking so much longer than she expected
She felt thrown away She felt used up She felt abandoned She felt weak
Her heart ached day and night She felt like the pain would never go away
She hid her true feelings sometimes They said she was phony
They said it would never last They ganged up against her sometimes
They did not appreciate her sacrifices They did not even see her sacrifices
She felt scattered They said she was not smart enough She felt left behind
They said she did not deserve it They said she deserved it
She felt like everything was going on without her She felt terribly lost
She wasn't always proud of the way she behaved She freaked out sometimes
She felt overwhelmed She was impatient They said she was not pretty enough
They said she was not skinny enough She felt unworthy sometimes
She sometimes felt like she was not pretty enough or skinny enough or smart enough
She hid out sometimes She sometimes did the wrong things She felt trapped
They said that she was trapped They said that she was not allowed to do that
She often ate until she could not feel She often drank until she could not feel
She felt bad They said it was too late They said it was too expensive
They said it was too darn weird They said it had been done before
It had been done before, but not like she was gonna do it She procrastinated a lot
She felt like she had too much to do before she could start
She was really afraid to start She had so many things on her plate
She was cautious She had a hard time expressing herself
It was very hard to see the good things some days She was scared to try again
She sometimes didn't feel important enough She had been lied to
She sometimes told herself mean things They were mean
They told her that it wasn't worth it They said she was a fraud
She wasn't sure if it would work She knew she had to fight for it
She was tired of fighting She knew it would be difficult
She fell down a few times She sometimes felt like she was not good enough
She had fallen on her face before, and it hurt She lost everything
She felt like a failure She was often depressed She felt attacked
It seemed that everything was a battle It sometimes seemed that all was lost
Things seemed bleak Life was very hard at times
She sometimes told herself that she would start tomorrow It seemed futile
She was out of groceries again She felt jaded and cynical
Everyone in her life seemed to leave The sky was grey and gloomy again
She hated her whole wardrobe Her family was dysfunctional
She had insomnia The doctor called with bad news Her wallet was empty

The economy was in the toilet She burned dinner again She got her tax bill
Her pants were too small that week There were wars all over the world
The lady at the grocery store was in a bad mood She had a crummy old car
Her kids spilled grape juice on her favorite tablecloth Her computer crashed
Everyone had a bigger house Her checking account was empty again
They were out of chocolate Her gas tank was on empty She was laid off
Her husband was laid off She was spending another weekend alone
Her kids were talking back She lost her temper She was running late
Someone used up all the hot water She had way too much on her to-do list
She had to bring store-bought cupcakes to the school party
Her lawn was too long Her hair was getting gray Her roots needed to be colored
She was in desperate need of a pedicure... and a manicure Her back hurt
She couldn't find her Spanx The neighbor's dog barked all night
She had another bad date She wasted her money on a dumb book
She had to go out of town Her flight was delayed Her baseboards were dusty
Her furniture was old and out of date Then there was global warming
Her face was falling Her hips were getting wider She couldn't find her lipstick
She forgot to put mascara on both eyes She needed glasses She had hot flashes
She had cellulite She served dinner on paper plates sometimes
She sometimes wore socks that didn't match She was domestically challenged
She compared her worst parts to others' best parts Her purse was a mess
She didn't always clean up her messes She was crabby on a moment's notice
She hid chocolate in random places just in case Her bum jiggled when she walked
Her homemade bread was shaped funny She sang off key Her boss was mean
She was addicted to reality TV She was behind on some of her bills
Her dog was old and crippled She was getting old and crippled
She was stuck in the eighties   She was quite disorganized at times
She had a thousand emails to reply to She was so late
She avoided housework and did other things all day She had to suffer sometimes
She did anything to avoid exercising She looked weird when she danced
She didn't have enough room in her house for everything
She had boxes in her garage and couldn't even remember what was in them
She heard all sorts of crazy and negative stuff on the news
She had wild ideas She failed sometimes She got off-track sometimes
She wanted to quit sometimes She came in last place
It was scary to think about doing it alone Not everyone appreciated her efforts
Not everyone understood her efforts She was afraid of hurting others
The odds were not looking good in the world Everyone was so grouchy
Others had tried the same thing and failed She had too much work
It didn't turn out as well as she expected They kept throwing more work at her
They expected too much to be done in too short a time She felt fat She felt old
She felt uninspired at times She felt boring at times She felt bored at times
She sometimes felt like she would never fit in She felt odd
Her recipes didn't always turn out She did not always read the directions
She gave up and ate fast food in her car sometimes She was so frustrated
Sometimes things just ended up in a disastrous mess They wouldn't help
Her marriage needed work Her closet was a mess She wanted to quit
No one seemed to listen to her ideas She doubted herself sometimes
She didn't feel put-together like everyone she saw on the internet
Life felt so tedious sometimes Her faith wasn't as strong as it used to be
She didn't have enough money to do the things she wanted to do   They left her out
Her work seemed pointless She couldn't kick her addiction She felt incapable
People could be so mean   The world scared her sometimes

61

she kept loving anyway
she kept dreaming anyway
she kept teaching anyway
she forgave anyway
she kept building anyway
she survived it anyway
she listened to her heart anyway
she stayed anyway
she did her best anyway
she was kind anyway
she protected it anyway
she kept singing anyway
she kept trying anyway
she reached out anyway
she got back up anyway
she did the right thing anyway
she was brave anyway
she kept creating anyway
she saw goodness anyway
she felt blessed anyway
she was generous anyway
she put herself into it anyway
she kept practicing anyway
she held tight anyway
she got back up anyway
she forgave herself anyway
she let it go anyway
she stayed on her path anyway
she was accepting anyway
she kept smiling anyway
she was patient anyway
she was happy anyway
she kept going anyway
she served them anyway
she was honest anyway
she kept seeing the good anyway
she shared her heart anyway
she accepted help anyway
she tried new things anyway
she survived it anyway
she felt fortunate anyway
she embraced change anyway
she made time anyway
she listened anyway
she dressed up anyway
she took care of herself anyway
she showed up anyway
she kept studying anyway

she kept loving them anyway
she kept teaching them anyway
she kept trying anyway
she kept climbing anyway
she kept dreaming anyway
she kept building anyway
she kept helping anyway
she kept sharing anyway
she stayed true anyway
she reached her goals anyway
she kept making goals anyway
she believed in herself anyway
she believed the truth anyway
she kept doing her best anyway
she loved them anyway
she tried again anyway
she kept learning anyway
she stayed on her path anyway
she made a difference anyway
she kept creating anyway
she spread hope anyway
she found beauty anyway
she created happiness anyway
she stayed happy anyway
she kept dancing anyway
she kept singing anyway
she enjoyed life anyway
she experienced miracles anyway
she reached out anyway
she spread happiness anyway
she forgave them anyway
she forgave herself anyway
she loved herself anyway
she made big plans anyway
she broke free anyway
she spread her wings anyway
she soared through life anyway
she blessed them anyway
she tried again anyway
she felt blessed anyway
she gave thanks anyway
she loved life anyway
she practiced kindness anyway
she did it anyway
she did it anyway
she did it anyway
she did it anyway
she did it anyway

JOURNALING QUESTIONS

1. Where am I tired of making excuses?

2. What do I need to be brave about?

3. What things have I already overcome, that give me strength and experience to continue overcoming new things that come along in life?

4. What will happen if I don't do it anyway?

5. What do I want to be the next chapter of my story?

6. How do I want my story to end?

7. What do I want to be known for in my life?

8. What is the legacy I want to leave?

9. What is the most important choice I need to make right now?

10. What do I commit to doing anyway?

Making &
Keeping
Boundaries

From here on out you get to decide how close other people and situations get to come to your Soul House. After doing all of the restoration you have been doing, it may feel like you don't ever want to take the risk of allowing anyone else into your life. You may even have tremendous apprehension about making boundaries with those who are in your life now, so much so that you are willing to let them keep trampling inside of your Soul House rather than having to deal with them in a new way.

Making and keeping boundaries does not have to cause turmoil in your life. It is not an act of aggression or something "mean" that you do to others.

Making boundaries is about figuring out how much space you need between yourself and another person to be able to have a healthy relationship, a relationship that accepts each person exactly as they are & does not need any person to be someone else...including ourselves.

Making and keeping boundaries is actually

a brave act of unconditional love.

We first need to take personal resposiblity for creating our boundaries and then explore how to keep ourselves safe based on our own personality, strengths and weaknesses, experiences and circumstances. Once we know what needs to be kept safe and sacred and whole...we can start to explore how close another human being or situation or experience is allowed to come into our life, our thoughts and our decision-making process.

Once we learn to have good boundaries, we can truly forgive everyone for everything...because we know we are safe from anyone's actions, and we do not expect them to change in order for us to feel whole.

Your Soul House is a sacred place. It is a place that is valuable and important. It needs to be protected. No matter how much others love us, they cannot make our boundaries for us...this is something that we have to be brave enough and diligent enough to do for ourselves. Once we know the truth about who we are...we've got to treat ourselves that way. When we treat ourselves with respect and value, others will treat us with respect and value. When they don't, they are not a good match for us, and we have to make stronger boundaries. Making and keeping boundaries is one of the most important skills we can ever learn.

Some people must be sent to the moon...

It is an enormous honor for anyone to ever be allowed to come anywhere near our Soul House, let alone know where it is. We must guard our souls in the way we would guard anything that is priceless and valuable and irreplacable. We must not allow just anyone to have access to our souls, to have influence on our souls and to speak to our souls in an influential way.

When we make and keep good boundaries, we can love just about anyone else by putting our interactions and our relationship with them in a far-away place that does not have the power to affect us, hurt us or destroy us. We can decide whether someone is allowed to come all the way to our figurative sidewalk or if we must figuratively meet them across town at a coffee shop. Sometimes we have to put others all the way "on the moon" and love them from there.

When the actions and words of others are toxic, disrespectful and hurtful, they become moon people. They can be exactly who they are and say exactly what they want to say and it will never affect us...they are too far away. We can love them and wish them well from that far away, and most importantly, we can do what is best for our own souls. We let others own their actions and their words and the consequences that come with them. We do the same for our-selves. Boundaries are good for everyone.

How do we know how close to allow someone into our lives, minds, hearts and souls? How do we know how strong of a boundary we need? A great way to identify the effect someone has on us is to ask ourselves how those in our lives handle our strengths and our weaknesses, our good times and our hard times. Those who protect us where we are weak and celebrate us where we are strong get to be closer in our lives. Those who poke at us, make fun of us and point out where we are weak and exploit us, use us and minimize us where we are strong do not get to come close to our souls.

JOURNALING QUESTIONS

1. Who do I want to call when something good happens?

2. Who do I want to hide the good things in my life from?

3. Who helps me most where I am weak?

4. Who loves to keep me weak where I am weak?

5. Who makes fun of me where I am weak?

6. Who celebrates me where I am strong?

7. Who keeps my sacred things sacred and confident?

8. Who quietly helps me in the places where I lack?

9. Who believes in my dreams and ideas?

10. Who shuts down my dreams and ideas?

11. Who is good and loyal to my beloveds?

12. Who condemns and criticizes my beloveds?

13. Who gossips about others to me?

14. Who sticks up for others?

15. Who would I trust no matter what?

16. Who would I never be able to trust?

Living With Boundaries

Broken people are often addicted to reactions and the power that they feel when they are able to produce strong reactions from others. When we are feeling strong reactions to the behaviors of others who are in our lives, rather than being able to calmly respond, we need to question the motives of others concerning an addiction to reactions. We also need to question our own need to have strong reactions to their behaviors.

It's hard to realize that we may just be playing into another's addiction to reactions by fueling their need for our reaction. The stronger and more out-of-control reaction they can get from us, the more we are fueling their need.

If you feel like someone is constantly trying to push your buttons, this is a person that you probably need to create some strong boundaries with. Once we stop reacting to situations, relationships and people that trigger us to feel powerless or defensive....we are able to take our power back.

When relating to another person, ask yourself if you are feeling compelled to give a response or a reaction. Reactions are fueled with emotion...and most of the time have not been thought through. Responses are calm answers that have been thought through and are completely under control, without fired up emotion. It is always okay if you need to let another person know that you need some time to respond. Whether it is a question or an interrogation, whether it is someone giving their opinion..you have the right to take as much time as you need to give a response that you feel good about.

It is a good idea to give yourself as much time as you need to feel in control of yourself, to feel like you can stand up for yourself and to feel like you can tell the truth with love and confidence. Just because someone is trying to push our buttons or is disrespectful and lacks boundaries, this does not mean that we have to react at the same level of behavior. We can choose to respond in a way that shows respect for ourselves and our boundaries.

We can also choose to not respond at all.

When we stop reacting to behavior that is offensive to our Soul House, often the offender will step up their game and try even harder to push our buttons to get an even stronger reaction. This is the time that we must stay firm in our boundaries and teach others what is okay with us and what is not. When we decide to stop fueling the reaction addiction of another, eventually this person will move on to someone else who will fuel them with reactions. We need to remember that we are not doing anyone any favors to continue to put up with or even welcome their unwanted behavior. No one likes to be bullied and poked at. No one likes to have their buttons pushed. When we refuse to tolerate destructive behavior, we help another to see that there are better ways to be in relationships. We help others learn to treat each other with love and respect. You cannot control others, but you can control how you respond.

We need to expect that those who have been benefiting from our lack of boundaries will often not be pleased when we start to live with boundaries. Sometimes they will even make us feel like we are bad or selfish for putting a limit on what is okay and what is not okay with us.

One of the most common things you may hear is....

"You've changed"

...and rather than doing what we usually do....cowering and feeling bad and asking what we can do to please them again....the very best response we can give is a loving and honest response where we completely own our behavior and simply say....

"Oh yes, I have changed...thank you for noticing...it has been a lot of work."

Choosing to Go Where the Peace is

It's all your choice now. You get to choose from now on whether to leave the light of truth on in your life or to walk in the dark. You get to choose to connect to your Truthteller and your Restoration Team. You get to choose whether to tell yourself stories about your experiences or whether to keep the wisdom you earned from them and let go of the rest. You get to choose to give yourself what you need. You get to choose to do it anyway. You get to choose to go where the peace is.

Today is day one of the rest of your life.

Today is day one. You get to begin this day making choices that are based in the truth of who you are. And guess what? Tomorrow is day one all over again. You get new opportunities every day to make the choices that will lead you to the places that you most want to go...the places you are meant to go.

No one can make your choices for you. You get to take complete responsibility for the rest of your life...for your actions, for your reactions, for your moods and for your thoughts. You are not powerless. You are powerful!!

Remember that a very good life is made up of lots of little choices, day after day. A good choice can make a good moment, which will lead to a good day...and day after day, more good choices will lead to a good month, and then to a good year. Beautiful choices moment by moment are what make a beautiful life.

DECISION MAKING QUESTIONS

1. Am I making this decision based on old beliefs or on the truth I know now?
2. Am I doing this from my heart or am I trying to please someone else?
3. Will making this decision bring me peace or stress me out?
4. Will making this decision help me grow into who I want to become?
5. Is this a decision that honors my potential, or does it fear my potential?
6. Would I be settling for second best if I made this decision?
7. Am I willing to live with all of the consequences of this decision?
8. Am I willing to do the scary and tedious things this decision requires?
9. Can I joyfully and thankfully work with those involved in this decision?
10. Will this decision inspire me to be my very best self every day?
11. Will I be appreciated and accepted exactly as I am if I make this decision?
12. Will I be taking the best care of my body and soul if I make this decision?
13. Will this choice challenge me or keep me comfortable?
14. Will this choice keep me stuck where I don't want to be?
15. Will this choice end up with the results I am truly seeking?
16. Will I be proud of this decision five years from now?
17. Am I making this decision from a brave and noble part of myself?
18. Am I making this decision from fear or from faith?
19. Is this what I really really want in my life?
20. Will others be able to control my decisions and time?
21. Am I being treated with kindness and respect by everyone involved?
22. Will I have to go into any kind of debt if I make this decision?
23. Will this hurt my family in any way?
24. Is this decision centered around my highest personal values?
25. Will I have to hide this decision from anyone I love & respect?
26. Am I going to find joy and fun from the results of this decision?
27. Do I want this decision to be part of the story of my life?
28. Would I be okay if young people followed in my footsteps with this decision?
29. Is this decision causing me to give up anything more precious than this decision is?
30. Will I be able to keep my promises to those I love if I make this decision?
31. Will I have time to rest and recharge if I make this decision?

When
Rough Days
Happen

There are still going to be days when you forget every single good thing you have ever learned, and when you want to fall back on default behaviors like eating a whole box of ice cream or charging up your credit card or drinking a whole bottle of wine. Rough days happen to all of us no matter how much soul work we have done.

On these days, we still have to honor our sadness or our anger or our exhaustion...we've got to listen to it and hear it out. Then we have to use the tools we worked so hard to learn and build. We have to prepare for rough days. One of the best ways to prepare for them is to expect that they will happen as a natural part of life and not beat ourselves up or feel like we've failed when they do happen.

Spend a little bit of time thinking through how you will handle rough days and make a plan...tell yourself that you are equipped, that you are on your own side, and that you will continue to protect your soul, especially on the rough days. You will know what to do. Go where the peace is.

It's a good idea to make yourself a "Rough Day Book"...a manual for you to read on the days when everything is wrong and you feel like you are going crazy. You could even have a "Rough Day Box" filled with things that make you feel better and help you focus on what is true.

Inside of your book, write out the following journaling prompts and finish the sentence stems:

What are my default behaviors when I am having a rough time?
What do I turn to that makes me feel worse?
What do I need to stay away from when I am having a rough time?
What are the triggers that bring on a rough time in my life?
What are some lies that are more exaggerated when I am having a rough time?

I feel better when I spend time doing...
I feel better when I spend time creating...
I feel better when I focus on...
I feel better when I spend time with...
I feel better when I reach out to...
I feel better when I tell the truth about...
I feel better when I focus on restoring...
I feel better when I protect...
I feel better when I make time for...
I feel better when I listen to...
I feel better when I eat...
I feel better when I see...
I feel better when I think about...
I feel better when I stop to...
I feel better when I talk to...
I feel better when I step away from...

Remember...rough days happen and you will make it through them!

Honoring Your Journey

It is so important to honor our rites of passage. This restoration journey you have taken deserves an honoring ceremony. We need to make a big deal of getting rid of what doesn't belong. It is time to burn your burn book! It is time for saying goodbye to what we no longer need, of thanking our experiences and lessons that life brought us and of welcoming and calling in what is to come. Your life deserves a ceremony & celebration...give yourself the things you need.

It is time to celebrate yourself, your homecoming, your victory. You made it. You deserve a medal as you come through the finish line of this journey. Please honor yourself in a special way.

IDEAS FOR HONORING YOUR JOURNEY:

- Burn Book: As you burn your Burn Book, tell it that you mean it; it's time
  for it to go. Build a safe fire in a safe fire receptacle and watch your
  Burn Book burn until it is ashes. Say goodbye to those lies once again.
- Write a 'Letter to Your Old Life', thanking it for the lessons it has taught
  you (see the following page for a sample letter). Plant a tree on top of the
  'Letter to Your Old Life' and invite it to grow into something else, thriving
  and moving on.
- Make or purchase a medal for yourself and have a medal ceremony.

77

Dear Old Life,

Today is the day, dear friend, that I finally lay you to rest. I have grown sick and tired of dragging you around, and I am certain that you have grown sick and tired of being dragged around, unable to move forward.

I am letting go of all the parts of you that have lived their life cycle and served their purpose, and I am allowing those parts to now move forward into their new purpose of becoming wisdom, experience, and fertile compost to grow my beautiful life into a healthy, thriving force for good and joy.

I'm sorry I have dragged you around for so long when you were ready to go. I am sorry I have not allowed you to become what you are meant to become next.

Today is the day.

I love you and I thank you. You have given me so many good and wonderful experiences. You have grown me into the woman I am today. I will always have the lessons you have taught me and the beautiful memories, as well as the good and necessary relationships and experiences. Those are the things that will be forever in my heart.

Today I am letting go of every regret, every mistake, every betrayal, every hurt, every messy ending, every disappointment, every attachment, every expectation, every failure, every label.

I am allowing this day to be day ONE of the rest of my life.

I am also giving myself the grace of allowing ANY day and EVERY day for the rest of my life to be DAY ONE OF THE REST OF MY LIFE.

I am opening my clasped hands and letting it all go... I am leaving my hands open to receive and embrace my brand new life.

I know that you will grow into a beautiful, thriving, living force and I invite you and support you in doing that. I am excited for you. I thank you for moving forward into your new life and purpose... I am doing the same.

Thank you for every single thing. I needed you, I appreciate you, I love you, I forgive you,

I wish you all the best.

Made in United States
Troutdale, OR
03/30/2024